MW01277600

The ABC's Lessons of Love

Sermon on the Mount ...for children

Written by Francine M. O'Connor
Illustrated by Kathryn Boswell

Catechetical Advisers:
The Redemptorists

LIGUORI
PUBLICATIONS

One Liguori Drive
Liguori, Missouri 63057-9999
(314) 464-2500

Imprimi Potest:
James Shea, C.SS.R.
Provincial, St. Louis Province
The Redemptorists

Imprimatur:
Monsignor Maurice F. Byrne
Vice Chancellor, Archdiocese of St. Louis

ISBN 0-89243-345-0

Copyright © 1991, Liguori Publications
Printed in U.S.A.

All rights reserved. No part of this booklet may be reproduced, stored in a retrieval system, or transmitted without the written permission of Liguori Publications.

Cover design by Chris Sharp

Contents

Note for Parents and Teachers

In planning this booklet, we hoped to create a sort of "mini-catechism" of the major teachings of Christ and present them in brief but enjoyable story form for children. After reading over the four gospels in search of some of the major Christian truths, we selected Matthew's Sermon on the Mount for two important reasons. First, the entire Gospel of Matthew is essentially a teaching gospel. A more important persuasion, however, came from the discovery that Matthew had already done our work for us by compiling Christ's teachings into one remarkable sermon.

While both Matthew and Luke present the Sermon in their Gospels, Matthew's version contains 107 verses. Of these, 29 are found in Luke's version, 47 have no parallel in Luke, and 34 are scattered in other places in Luke's Gospel (*The Gospel of Matthew, Volume 1* by William Barclay). Thus, biblical scholars agree that Matthew's Sermon contains a summary of Christ's consistent teachings to his disciples.

Each story is followed by an activity, game, or project to help parents and teachers solidify the story's lesson in an experiential way.

And, by the way, we also hope that as the children learn about Jesus, they will have a bit of fun in the process.

Francine O'Connor

A Mountainside Lesson in Love

(MATTHEW 5-7)

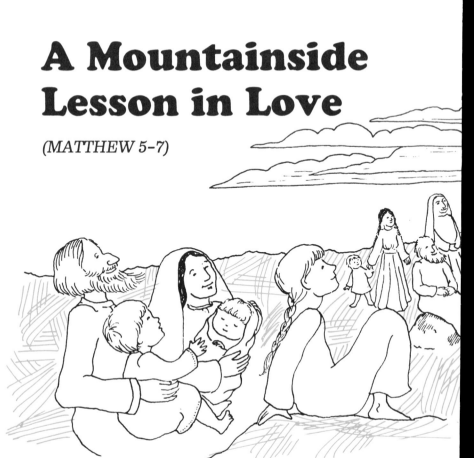

When Jesus was teaching on the mountainside,
the people came to hear him from far and wide.
He spoke about blessings and he spoke about light,
and he spoke of a love that will bring delight.

He said if you obey his commandments of love,
you'll be loved by his Father in heaven above.
And he said to love your enemy too,
not just the people who are kind to you.

If someone asks to share your toys with you,
share your toys, your games, and your friendship too.
Whenever you fight with a brother or a friend,
you must make up your quarrel before the day's end.

If you're feeling angry
toward your neighbor today,
don't try to get even.
That just doesn't pay.
"An eye for an eye"
is the wrong kind of rule.
Forgiveness is the lesson
taught in Jesus' school.

Now loving those who hurt you
is quite hard to do,
and not everyone can love
in this way, it is true.
But we remember Jesus,
who answered love's call
by dying on the cross because
he cared for us all.

There were many other things that Jesus had to say
on the mountainside in Galilee, so very far away.
His everlasting words we remember to this day.
They comfort and guide us and help us as we pray.

Learning From Jesus

Read this booklet slowly, one story at a time.
You will learn many things about Jesus.
You will learn many things
about being a good Christian.

Here are some things Jesus said on the mountaintop. On the lines below the quote, write something you can do this week to follow his words.

(If you don't know what some of the words mean, ask a grownup or your big sister or brother to help you.)

"Blessed are the peacemakers."

_____

_____

"You are the light of the world."

_____

_____

"Whoever is angry with his brother will be liable to judgment."

_____

_____

"Give to the one who asks of you."

_____

_____

"Love your enemies."

_____

_____

Be Happy

(MATTHEW 5:1-12)

When Jesus was in Galilee,
he taught the crowds who gathered there.
He had many wonderful things to say,
and all the people were eager to hear.
He knew that some of the people were poor
and that some of them were sad.
But all of them loved God a lot,
and they tried hard not to be bad.
AND HE SMILED A GENTLE JESUS SMILE.

BE HAPPY! he told them, all you who love God
more than the things that you own.
The very best love you can ever know
is the love that you feel for God alone.

BE HAPPY! he told them,
all you who are kind
to your neighbors and
family and friends,
like the times when
you help wash the car
or dry the dishes
when mealtime ends.

BE HAPPY! he told them,
when you try so hard
to do the things that you know are right.
Even when other kids are doing wrong,
you always keep God's commandments in sight.

BE HAPPY! he told them, all you who forgive
when someone hurts you or makes you sad.
For our Father is such a forgiving God,
and following his way will make you glad.

BE HAPPY! he told them, when mean-hearted folks
make fun of those good things you do.
God knows what a wonderful person you are
and has planned a special reward for you.

He told them again and again and again,
no matter what hardships you go through.
BE HAPPY! GOD LOVES YOU! for you are his own.
God made heaven and earth just for you.

What Jesus taught then, he teaches today.
BE HAPPY — for you have a loving Father
who knows when you're sad, hears when you pray,
and is filled with joy when you love one another.

Make Someone Happy Today!

Parent or teacher: You will need a large face that is happy when turned one way, sad when inverted. Keep it simple so the kids can copy it.

Would you like to help Jesus spread the happy news about God? Here is one way to do it.

1. Make HAPPY/SAD buttons for your friends. Cut a piece of heavy cardboard into a circle. Draw a HAPPY/SAD face on each cardboard circle. Tape a safety pin to the back of the face.
2. If a friend is sad, pin the button upside down. Make that person laugh or smile so you can turn the button over.
3. See if you can keep all your friends' buttons right side up by making them happy every day.

God's Gift of Light

(MATTHEW 5:13-16)

One night after dark, when Tim was in bed,
he saw a big monster down by his feet.
"Mother!" he called in his loudest voice,
and he buried his head under the sheet.

His mother came in and he pointed one finger
at the monster rising way up in the air.
But his mother laughed and turned on the lamp —
it was only his robe hanging there.

After that, Tim was a little bit scared
to go to sleep all alone in his room.
So his mother switched his night-light on,
and it brightened the shadows and gloom.

The very next morning
when Tim woke up,
the whole room was sunny
and bright.
Out of his window
he could see God's world,
all shimmering in the
sun's special light.

Light helps us to see where we're going;
light keeps us from being afraid;
light shows us the way things really are
and brightens the gifts that God made.

Jesus told the people on the mountain that day
to be lights for the people they know.
Think about light, about Jesus, and you
and brighten the world with your own special glow.

Let Your Light Shine!

Jesus said, "You are the light of the world."
Jesus lives in your heart.
The light of Jesus' love
shines in your heart.
Your light is LOVE — a Jesus kind of love!
Let it shine!

Here are several ways
to be a light for others.
Choose one and let
your light burn brightly.

Ask God in prayer to help you be a light.
Give Mom or Dad a hug — just because.
Visit an elderly or shut-in neighbor.
Learn a Jesus song and teach it to your family.

Clean up your room
without being asked.

Write a letter to someone
who's far away.

Following Jesus

(MATTHEW 5:17-20)

It's a whole lot of fun to play Follow the Leader
when Jesus, our Brother, is leading the game.
You just have to remember some things that he did,
then try in your own life to do the same.

Remember how Jesus would walk for miles
to help those who were weary or feeling sad?
Now you follow Jesus. Play helper today.
Do something special to make someone glad.

Remember how Jesus always
loved the poor?
How he said that
God's kingdom
was theirs?
Now you
follow Jesus.
Try checking
your toys
and see what
you have
you can share.

Remember how Jesus said "Love your neighbor" in the story of the poor beaten man in the street? Now you follow Jesus. Try helping your neighbor or sharing a smile with the people you meet.

Remember how Jesus
would go off alone
to be closer to God
when he wanted to pray?
Now you follow Jesus.
Go off by yourself
and tell God the Father
all about your day.

Follow the Leader is the best game to play,
letting Jesus lead you wherever, whenever.
If you follow him all the days of your life,
you will play it with him in heaven forever.

A "Following Jesus" Poster

Make a poster to remind everyone in the family to
follow Jesus every day. Follow these steps to make
your poster:

1. Across the top of a large piece of poster paper, print
   the words WE ARE FOLLOWING JESUS. Use bright
   colored markers for your printing.
2. Trace the footprints of every member of the family
   on your poster. Print the name of each person
   inside his or her own footprint. Make it look like the
   footprints are following one another.

3. Search through magazines to find pictures of people doing kind things for others. Cut out the pictures and scatter them around your poster with the footprints.
4. Hang your poster where everyone in the family can see it every morning to remind them to follow Jesus that day.

Don't Get Mad, Get Glad!

(MATTHEW 5:21-25)

When Jimmy was angry
at his best friend, Joe,
he muttered and sputtered
and carried on so
about something Joe said
to him at school,
and he told everybody,
"That Joe is a fool."

On Sunday morning,
as it all came to pass,
Jimmy was still angry
when he left for Mass.
His mother said, "Jimmy,
just stop being mad
and come to Jesus with
a heart that is glad."

When Jimmy saw Joe walking down the aisle,
he offered his hand and gave him a smile.
"I'm sorry," he said, "for getting so mad.
Fighting with you really made me feel sad."

As they walked down that aisle arm in arm,
the feeling they shared was friendly and warm.
Everyone smiled when they looked at those two,
and I'm certain that Jesus was smiling too.

Jesus said, "Please don't bring your gifts to me
when you're angry at someone else, you see.
Go first to that person and make amends,
for I want my people to always be friends."

What a loving lesson Jesus taught that day
on the mountain in Galilee far, far away.
Because he feels sad when his people are mad,
Jesus gave us the secret of how to be glad.

When Loving Is Hard to Do

Here are some things that you can do
when loving others is hard for you.

**WHEN YOU HAVE HAD A FIGHT
WITH YOUR FRIEND:**

1. Make a list of all the fun things you and your friend
   have done together.
2. Choose the one thing you enjoyed most and plan to
   do it again.
3. Call your friend to come over and share the fun.

WHEN YOU ARE PUNISHED FOR SOMETHING YOU DID:

1. Make up a story in your mind. You are the parent and your mother or your father is the child. Imagine that your make-believe child did the same thing you are being punished for.
2. How did it feel to have your make-believe child disobey you?
3. Write a note to your parent or parents to say you're sorry.

WHEN SOMEONE IS MEAN TO YOU:

1. Pray for the person who was mean.
2. Try to think of some good things about that person.
3. Remember how it feels to be forgiven. In your heart, forgive the person who was mean — **and don't try to get even.**

God Loves a Secret

(MATTHEW 6:1-4)

There was a little girl with
pretty mouth a-curl
forever in a happy secret smile.
What makes her always glad?
Why is she never sad?
I couldn't help but wonder
all the while.

This happy little child,
so contented and so mild,
knew a secret that I really
had to know.
For if I knew what she knew,
I'd be smiling too,
and on my face would be
that happy glow.

Early every day she would kneel down to pray,
then go searching all around her little room
to find a game or toy that had given her some joy
or a book to brighten someone else's gloom.

At school she'd look around till finally she found
a boy or a girl who looked a little sad.
When no one was around, she'd hide the toy she found
where the other child would find it and be glad.

I know it may seem strange, but I noticed quite a change
as the children in our class began to smile.
Sometimes they'd find a toy, sometimes a poem of joy
written by that lovely little child.

Her secret, I now know, came from Jesus long ago:
"Don't talk about the gifts you give away.
If only God and you know the kindnesses you do,
then God, who loves a secret, will repay."

And Jesus must be right, for I have found delight
spreading joy in this special Jesus way.
I find someone who's sad and make that person glad.
And the smile that's on my face is here to stay.

You'll be happy too if you do as Christians do
and become a secret giver every day.
Just find a bit of cheer to give to someone near,
then share it with the Father when you pray.

Be a Secret Giver

You can be a secret giver in your very own family.
Here are some gifts you can give.

WILDFLOWERS

If there are wildflowers growing
near your house, pick a
bouquet and secretly place it in
a glass of water. Place the
bouquet on the kitchen table
when no one is looking. (Be
sure they really are wildflowers,
though. Don't pick flowers out
of someone's yard without
asking permission.)

A DRAWING

Draw a happy smiling face. Color it with bright crayons or markers. Print I LOVE YOU! across the bottom of the picture. Leave it on someone's pillow.

SECRET CHORE

Clear the table or dust the furniture or pick up your toys and put them away. Do it when no one is looking. Watch your parents' faces when they see how nice everything looks.

Emily Boswell Hates Being Small

(MATTHEW 6:25-34)

Emily Boswell hates
being small.
She is sure that God
can't see her at all.
She stands on her tiptoes
to make herself tall.
That's how much Emily
hates being small.

Look around, Emily,
just look and see.
There are violets growing
under that tree.
God made each blossom
so perfectly,
and a violet is just
as small as can be.

And look in the branches over your head.
A wee baby bird is going to bed.
Tomorrow his mother will teach him to fly
on tiny blue wings that will carry him high.

31

Jesus said, "See how
the Father takes care
of the flowers in the field
and the birds in the air.
Think how much more
he will care about you,
watching over you always,
whatever you do."

God is a Father with enough love for all.
He makes some of us short and some of us tall.
He gives us the things that we need as we grow
and Jesus to teach what he wants us to know.

Feed God's Birds

Jesus said to see how the Father takes care of the birds of the air. Here's how you can help God care for the birds by feeding them every day.

1. Make a simple feeder by cutting a round hole in a plastic milk carton. Decorate the carton with bright colored markers.
2. Fill your feeder with breadcrumbs, birdseed, popcorn, small pieces of apple, or dry cereal.
3. Tie a string around the neck of the carton and hang it in a nearby tree.

You can also string popcorn like you do at Christmastime and hang that in the tree for the birds.

Knock, Knock, Jesus

(MATTHEW 7:7-11)

Knock, knock, Jesus. "Who is there?"
This is Wyatt, and here's my prayer.
I get good marks and I know I'll pass,
but I want to be the smartest one in class.

"I hear you, Wyatt, and your request.
I know you study and do your best.
But you don't have to get all A's for me.
You just have to be as good as you can be."

Knock, knock, Jesus. "Who is there?"
This is Gabriel with my special prayer.
I am too little for chores right now.
I'd like to help, but I don't know how.

"I hear you, Gabriel, and the words you pray.
Just see how you're growing every day.
Be patient, little friend, there's time to spare.
I will need a few years to answer your prayer."

Knock, knock, Jesus.
"Who is there?"
This is Judith and
here's my prayer.
Can you teach me
to be kind to others,
especially to my pesky
little brothers?

"I hear you, Judith,
and I know you try,
and you're getting better
as the days go by.
Just think of the love
that I give to you,
then give that love
to your brothers too."

Jesus said, "Knock and I will open the door,"
for he wants to answer all your prayers and more.
He helps you in all that you are trying to do,
as you grow in the way God has planned for you.

He also said, "Ask and I will give to you,"
and to that great promise he always is true.
To grow up Christian, you need a good guide.
That's why Jesus is always at your side.

Knocking for Others

You know that Jesus
hears and answers
your prayers.
Jesus said, "Knock and
it will be open to you."
This week, pray for the
needs of others.
Here are some ideas.

KNOCK FOR YOUR FAMILY

Ask Jesus to make you a happy and loving family every day.

KNOCK FOR YOUR FRIENDS

Ask Jesus to help a friend with his or her special problem.

KNOCK FOR THE POOR

Ask Jesus to take care of the poor. Ask him to help you find a way to help them too.

KNOCK FOR OUR LEADERS

Ask Jesus to guide our country's leaders in the very hard jobs they have to do. Ask him to make them kind and fair in their decisions.

God's Rule Is a Golden Rule

(MATTHEW 7:12)

Jesus said, Do to others what you would
like them to do to you.
He called this rule his GOLDEN RULE,
and here's how you can follow it through.

Just think about how good you feel
when Mom gives you a hug
and says, "I love you!"
God's golden rule says
hug her right back
and say to her,
"I love you too!"
GOD'S GOLDEN RULE
MEANS LOVE!

Think about how much fun you have
when your friends share their toys with you.
God's golden rule says it's even more fun
when you are sharing your own toys too.
GOD'S GOLDEN RULE MEANS FRIENDSHIP!

Think about
the happy surprise
when Grandma makes
something just for you.
God's golden rule
says it's your turn now
to make a love-present
for Grandma too.
GOD'S GOLDEN RULE
MEANS MAKING
OTHERS HAPPY!

GOLDEN means something shining and bright,
like a sunny summer day or a Christmas tree.
And a RULE is a law made from God's love
that helps us to be the best we can be.

So the golden rule is a bright shining way
to follow Jesus along the way.
Just think about something you really enjoy,
then do the same thing for someone today.

A Golden Ruler

Here is a "golden ruler" you can use to remind you to treat others as you would like to be treated.

Turn this page sideways and write on each line of the ruler one of the following ways to follow God's golden rule.

LOVE OTHERS
BE KIND
BE FAIR
SHARE A SMILE

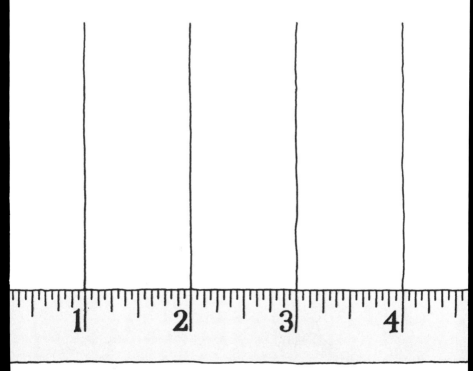

Sandcastles

(MATTHEW 7:24-28)

Nicholas built a castle all out of sand.
He worked in the hot summer sun for hours.
He shaped each wall carefully with his hands
and built bridges and tunnels and tall toppling towers.

Can you guess what happened to that castle so tall
when the tide came up to wash the beach clean?
Not a tunnel nor a tower
nor a bridge nor a wall
of Nicholas' sandcastle
was there to
be seen.

Jesus told the story of a very foolish man
who built a fine house on soft sandy ground.
When the rains came along and washed it away,
like Nicholas' castle, no sign could be found.

Well, that's how it will be for people who
build their whole lives on selfishness and greed.
They think money or toys or big fancy cars
will give them all the power they will need.

BUT God won't be with them when things go wrong,
and they won't have Jesus to talk to at night.
They won't have his help to make them strong,
and in the end, they'll be washed out of sight.

So let's build our lives on Jesus instead.
Following his way will make us be strong.
And like the man who built his house on a rock,
God will protect us when things go wrong.

Neither rain nor storm nor long scary nights
will make us forget about Jesus, our friend.
And in our last days God will welcome us home
to that place where happiness never ends.

A Rock Hunt

Here's a good way to remember that Jesus is your Rock.

1. Search for a large, smooth rock. Don't hurry your search. Check out rocks of interesting shapes until you find the one you like best.
2. Scrub your rock with a brush and dishwashing soap. Let the rock dry for about a day in bright sunlight.
3. With bright colored markers, print JESUS IS MY ROCK! on your rock. Decorate the rock with flowers or designs to make it look pretty.
4. Place your rock somewhere in your room to remind you of how strong and solid your love for Jesus can be.

THE ABC's AUDIO/BOOK READ-ALONG PACKS
Produced by Redemptorist Pastoral Communications
**A special treat for kids — a fun, entertaining way
to learn about our faith. . .**

Francine O'Connor's best-loved *ABC* books are now available as
Read-along Packs. A lively reading of each book — enhanced by
sound effects and music — is recorded on individual audio
cassettes by actress Susie Wall. Each cassette comes with a copy
of the colorfully illustrated companion book.

THE ABC's OF THE SACRAMENTS. . .for children

This fun-filled, faith-filled way introduces kids to both familiar
and yet-to-be experienced sacraments. It touches on each of the
important elements of faith to help children understand God's
loving presence at baptism, Eucharist, and more. **$9.95**

THE ABC's OF THE TEN COMMANDMENTS
. . .for children

Children will love following along in the colorfully illustrated
book as they learn about the commandments through lively
stories like Don't Let the Grumpy Get You, The Town That Had
No Rules, Finders Keepers, and many others. **$9.95**

THE ABC's OF PRAYER. . .for children

Children will learn how prayer is our special way of com-
municating with God through verses like Communion Prayer
and Prayer Is Listening Too. They are also encouraged to pray
along with actual prayers-in-verse. **$9.95**

Order from your local bookstore or write to:
Liguori Publications
Box 060, Liguori, MO 63057-9999
For faster service call toll-free 1-800-325-9521, ext. 060.
(Please add $1.50 for postage and handling.)